SPORT

PLAYERS, GAMES & SPECTACLE

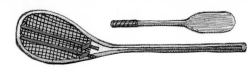

Series Editor:
David Salariya was born in Dundee, Scotland, where he studied illustration and printmaking, concentrating on book design in his post-graduate year. He later completed a further post-graduate course in art education at Sussex University. He has illustrated a wide range of books on botanical, historical, and mythical subjects. He has designed and created many new series of children's books for publishers in the U.K. and overseas. In 1989, he established his own publishing company, The Salariya Book Company Ltd. He lives in Brighton with his wife, the illustrator Shirley Willis.

Author:
Norman Barrett is a graduate of Oxford University. He planned and edited the 3,000-page partwork *The Game*, an encyclopedia of sports. He has written many books on sports, including *Purnell's Encyclopedia of Sport, Great Moments in Sport* and *Soccer: The Last 25 Years.* He lives and works in Edgware.

Consultant:
David Preston is a free-lance sports journalist who has contributed to many publications. He has edited a number of sports magazines, including *Winners* and *Countdown to the Summer Olympics.*

Series Editor	David Salariya
Senior Editor	Ruth Taylor
Book Editor	Vicki Power
Assistant Designer	Steve Longdale
Consultant	David Preston
Artists	Mark Bergin
	Ryz Hajdul
	Nick Hewetson
	John James
	Mark Peppé
	Gerald Wood

First published in the
United States in 1993

Franklin Watts, Inc.
95 Madison Avenue
New York, N.Y. 10016

© The Salariya Book Co Ltd MCMXCIII

Printed in Belgium

Artists
Mark Bergin p 6-7, p 8-9; **Ryz Hajdul** p 42-43; **Nick Hewetson** p 10-11, p 18-19, p 20-21, p 22-23, p 32-33; **John James** p 14-15; **Mark Peppé** p 24-25, p 26-27, p 28-29, p 30-31, p 38-39, p 40-41; **Gerald Wood** p 12-13, p 16-17, p 34-35, p 36-37.

Barrett, Norman S.
Sport : players, games, and spectacle / by Norman Barrett.
p. cm. – (Timelines)
Includes index.
ISBN 0-531-15262-6.
1. Sports – History – Juvenile literature. I. Title. II. Series: Timelines (Franklin Watts, Inc.)
GV571.B36 1993

TIMELINES
SPORT

PLAYERS, GAMES & SPECTACLE

Written by
NORMAN BARRETT

Created & Designed by
DAVID SALARIYA

FRANKLIN WATTS

New York • Chicago • London • Toronto • Sydney

CONTENTS

6 **ORIGINS OF SPORTS**
Spears and arrows, Running, Hunting, Bull leaping, Boxing, Hammer-throwing, Polo.

8 **ANCIENT GREECE**
Gatherings, Religious festivals, The first Olympics, Pancration.

10 **ANCIENT ROME**
Bread and circuses, Gladiators, The Colosseum, Circus Maximus, Bestiarii, The tepidarium.

12 **EAST AND WEST**
Martial arts, Self-defense, Aztecs, Mayas, Baggataway, Kyudo, Kendo, Sumo wrestling, Kite flying.

14 **MIDDLE AGES**
Knights, Jousting, Tournaments, Mob soccer, Archery.

15 **RENAISSANCE**
Leisure activities, Tennis, Palla, Real tennis, Fencing, Skating.

16 **MODERN SPORTS**
Kolven, Golf, Featheries, Pell-mell, Billiards, Coffeehouses, Cricket, Rowing, Early baseball, Tennis.

18 **ANIMALS**
Chariot racing, Hunting and shooting, Bullfighting, Fox hunting, Leaping contests, Tiger hunting.

20 **TEAM SPORTS**
Soccer, Baseball, Rugby, Women cricketers, Basketball.

22 **GATHERINGS**
First modern Olympics, Highland games, Wimbledon, Badminton.

24 **MAKING RULES**
Tenpin bowling, Queensberry rules, Fencing, Dueling.

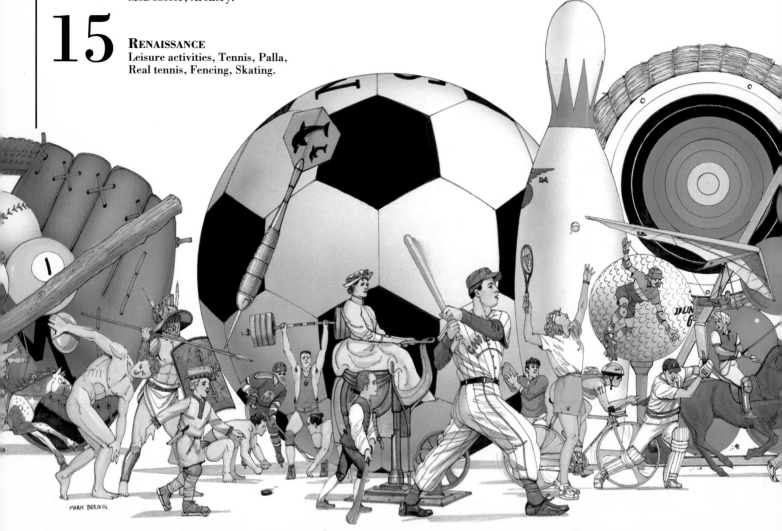

MARK BERGIN.

25 WHEELS
Bicycle racing, Penny-farthing, Car racing, Motorcycles.

26 WATER SPORTS
Swimming, Rowing, Diving, Sailing, Kayaks.

27 WINNING WOMEN
Tennis, Figure skating, Drag racing, Swimming the English channel.

28 HEROES
Superstars, Live radio, Paavo Nurmi, Babe Ruth, Professionals.

29 WORLD STAGE
International sports, Politics, Berlin Olympics, First World Cup.

30 WAR AND PEACE
The Iron Curtain, Racial prejudice, Advertising, Four-minute mile.

31 POWER GAMES
Football, Live television, Olympic water polo.

32 THE OLYMPICS
Munich '72, Terrorism, Boycotts, Olympic flame, Professionalism.

34 WINTER SPORTS
Skiing, Skating, Refrigerated rinks, Winter Olympics, Tobogganing, Ski-jumping, Bobsled, Ice hockey.

36 MODERN AGE
Big business, Sponsorhip, Advertising, Fallen idols.

38 SPEED
Sprinting, Drag racing, Golf, Records, Jai alai, Technology.

40 DRESS AND EQUIPMENT
Lycra, Silk, Sports clothes for women, Manufacturers, Racing cars.

42 TECHNOLOGY
Safety in sports, Victorian gym equipment, Making tennis rackets, Racing driver's outfit.

43 THE FUTURE
New Games, Earthball, Gladiators, Virtual reality.

44 TIMELINE

46 GLOSSARY

48 INDEX

ORIGINS OF SPORTS

△ AN EARLY SKIER, as illustrated in a 4000-year-old rock carving found in Norway. Skiing was a means of transportation rather than a sport.

THE EARLIEST PEOPLE had little time for sports, as their chief daily occupation was to find enough food to survive. But it was this very search for food that led to the first sporting activities. It was natural for people to run, jump, swim, and throw spears and arrows when hunting for food, warding off dangerous animals, and escaping from their enemies.

In ancient Egypt and other cultures, sports became an important part of the religious rites practiced to encourage the growth of crops and the return of spring. Often, a ball was used to represent the sun and its powers.

△ A 5000-YEAR-OLD VASE from northern Africa shows wrestlers grasping each other's loincloths.

▷ WOMEN DANCING and tossing balls in a scene from an ancient Egyptian tomb.

◁ RUNNING was practiced by ancient Egyptian pharaohs to show off their physical superiority and make them seem "godlike."

▷ HUNTING was a favorite sport in ancient Egypt. A nobleman uses a curved stick to hunt for birds.

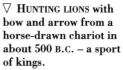

▽ HUNTING LIONS with bow and arrow from a horse-drawn chariot in about 500 B.C. – a sport of kings.

▽ WRESTLING AND FIGHTING with sticks in a contest to entertain the pharaoh and other nobility – taken from an ancient Egyptian carving (c.1160 B.C.).

△ BULL LEAPING was a favorite sport of the Minoans, who lived on Crete from c.3000 to c.1200 B.C.

◁ MEN AND WOMEN took part. The leaper would grab the horns of a charging bull, pull herself up, and turn a handspring over the animal's back, while her companion waited to steady her landing.

▽ BOXING was also popular with the Minoans. A young boy and girl are shown sparring.

Sports in ancient times probably provided the same satisfaction that it gives today. It not only amused people in their leisure time, but helped to relieve tension and overcome natural aggression. It was less destructive to compete in sports than in war - sports have often been described as "war without the shooting." Ancient cultures such as the Minoans, who lived in the Mediterranean from c.3000 B.C. to c.1200 B.C. were one of the least hostile of the early civilizations. Their bull leaping thrilled spectators and called for breathtaking skills and courage. Sporting contests emerged in northern Europe, too, where participants competed in contests of strength.

Sports also evolved from military training. Unarmed combat and horse-riding were probably first used in war.

▽ AT THE TAILTEANN GAMES of Ireland, in c.2000 B.C. competitors were judged on their strength. Men competed in hammer-throwing (*left*) and stone-tossing (*right*).

△▷ POLO began as a religious rite to promote crops. The ball, representing the sun, was a symbol of fertility. Polo originated in Persia, where it was sometimes played using enemy heads as balls (*right*).

ANCIENT GREECE

IN ANCIENT TIMES many great sports gatherings, or games, developed from religious festivals. The Greeks began to organize festivals in honor of their gods in about 1400 B.C. and some of these included sporting events. Hercules is said to have founded the Olympic Games in 776 B.C. to pay tribute to Zeus, king of the gods.

The ancient Greek Olympics were for men only. Women held their own games in honor of Hera, queen of the gods. At their height, the Games lasted five days and included javelin throwing and chariot racing.

Besides honoring the gods, the Greek Games celebrated manliness and power with events such as boxing and wrestling. Although victors received only a crown of leaves as a prize, they were showered with rewards in their hometowns. The community shared in the winner's glory and seemed mightier as a result.

△ A SPRINT of nearly 200 meters was the only event of the first Olympic Games in 776 B.C.

△ THE TORCH RACE was a relay held as a religious ritual - the "carrying of the sacred fire" - in local festivals.

△ "KERETIZEN," a type of hockey played in pairs, was one of many ball games played by the ancient Greeks.

▽ STARTING GATE used at the Isthmian Games. With one jerk, the starter released bars in front of each runner.

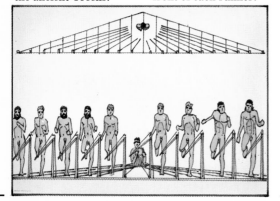

▽ OLYMPIA, the site of the ancient Greek Olympics, was chiefly a religious sanctuary, with temples and other holy buildings, as well as areas for sports.

△ THE RACE IN ARMOR was first included in the 65th Olympics (520 B.C.). In races of 400 or 800 meters, each runner wore a helmet and carried a shield.

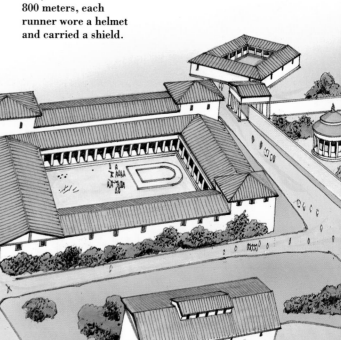

△ THROWING THE DISCUS.

△ THE JAVELIN came from war and hunting.

△ WEIGHT LIFTING was used in training.

△ BALL SKILL demonstrated by a Greek youth.

△ A JUDGE awards a victor his prize.

△ WOMEN TOOK PART in sports, but not in the Olympics.

△ LONG JUMPERS used weights as an aid.

▽ CHARIOT RACING was a spectacular sport.

▷ CHARIOT RACES were first held in 680 B.C.

A truce from all wars was called for the duration of the Olympic Games, which were open only to men from Greek city-states. Foreigners were not allowed to compete, and women were not even allowed to watch. From the 15th Games (720 B.C.), the runners ran naked. Later, none of the competitors wore clothes. Even trainers were obliged to go naked after 388 B.C., when a mother who had trained her son to victory was discovered at the Games, disguised as a man.

△ "PANCRATION" was an Olympic event - a form of wrestling in which the loser might be maimed or killed.

▽ THE TEMPLE OF ZEUS at Olympia is the columned building below. The stadium where races took place is on the right.

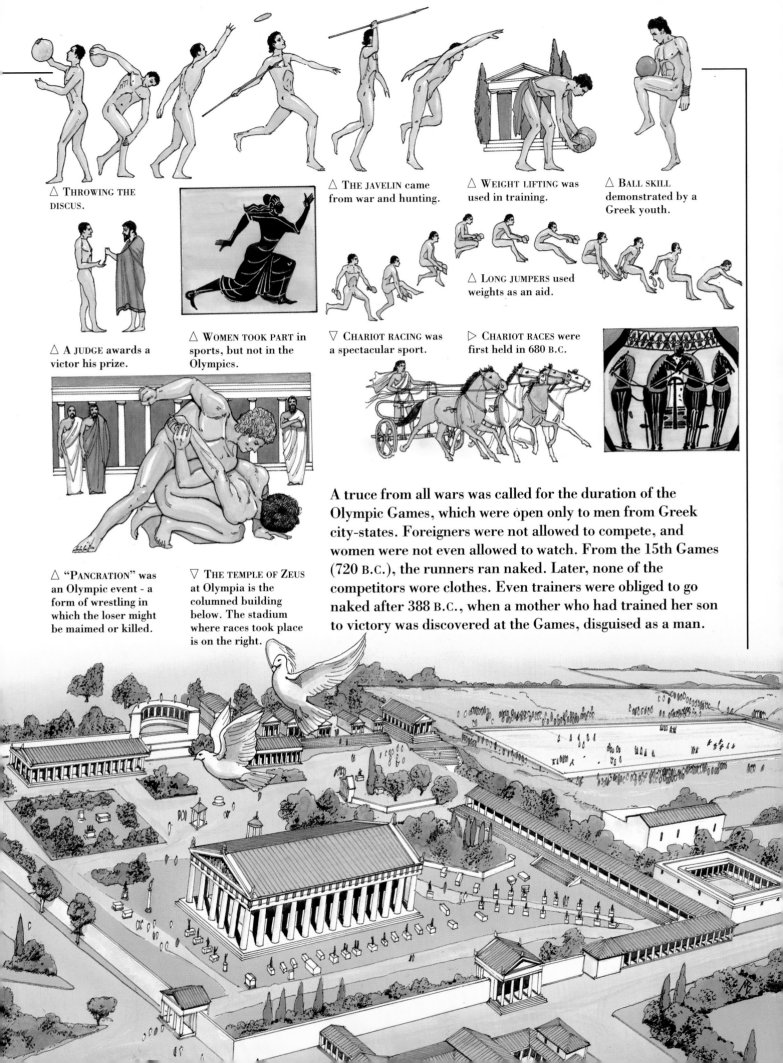

ANCIENT ROME

THE ROMAN EMPIRE reached its height in the first century A.D., when it covered much of Europe and the Middle East. Ordinary citizens enjoyed a great amount of leisure time - slaves did much of their work and 159 days of the year were holidays.

To keep people happy and avoid political unrest, the Roman emperors provided "bread and circuses." Bread was a free daily ration of wheat. Circuses were great free entertainments put on in huge outdoor arenas called amphitheaters. The most famous was the Colosseum in Rome. Nearly everyone, including slaves, women, and children, attended spectacles in the amphitheaters, where the entertainment was violent and bloody.

▷ GLADIATOR with sword and shield, fighting for the amusement of the people.

▽ A "THUMBS-DOWN" from the emperor meant death for the vanquished.

△ EXERCISE was a habit the Romans learned from the Greeks. They ran, wrestled, skipped, and played ball in gymnasia attached to the public baths.

▽ CHARIOT RACING was thrilling. Two-wheeled chariots, drawn by 2 to 8 horses, raced around the oval track.

▷ ROME'S CIRCUS MAXIMUS was the greatest chariot racing arena, holding 200,000 people and boasting shops, stalls, and toilets.

◁ HUGE PILLARS marked the turning points of the track, and lap markers kept the crowd informed of the progress of a race.

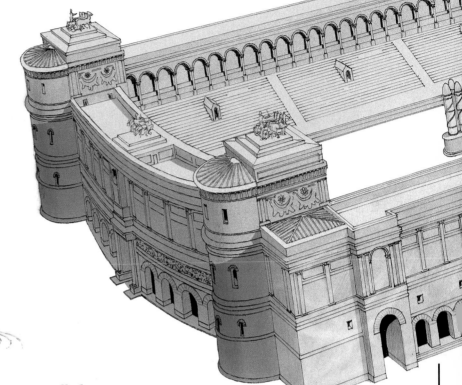

The men who fought in the amphitheaters were called gladiators (some women became gladiators, too, until this was outlawed in A.D. 200). Gladiators were slaves, criminals, or prisoners of war. They were armed and set against other criminals with less armor and Christians.

While they loved watching bloody entertainment, the Romans also enjoyed playing sports. Children played with hoops, tops, and balls. Adults exercised daily in gymnasia and bathed in the lavish public baths.

▷ A STATUE of a professional boxer based on a Roman mosaic of the first century A.D. He has a "caestus" (leather thongs) on his forearms.

▽ IN THE "TEPIDARIUM," or warm room, of the public baths, Romans enjoyed having their skin scraped clean.

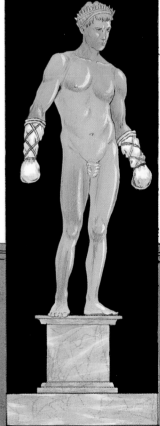

◁ CHRISTIANS, who were persecuted in ancient Rome, were thrown to the lions in an amphitheater for the entertainment of the people. Christianity later became the Empire's chief religion.

▷ THE "BESTIARII" were specially trained to fight wild animals. The bestiarii were armed and they "fed" condemned men to the starved beasts.

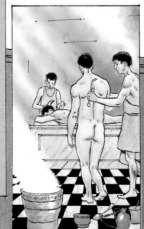

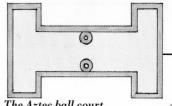

EAST AND WEST

The Aztec ball court.

△ PLAYERS in the Aztec ball game wore elbow and hip protectors.

SPORTS IN THE EAST AND WEST evolved independently of Europe and the Mediterranean. The Aztecs and Mayas of Central America played a ball game as a religious rite to promote growth. The Aztec game, called *tlachtli*, was played in a court shaped like a capital letter "I." The court represented the world, and the movement of the ball symbolized the sun or the moon. A goal was scored when one team managed to get the rubber ball into the opposing team's end of the court using only their elbows, hips, and knees. The game was won outright when one team passed the ball through a ring placed high above the court.

◁ THE LOSING CAPTAIN was beheaded by the winners if the ball was hit through the ring.

◁ IF A PLAYER placed the ball through the ring, he could claim spectators' clothes and jewelry as a reward.

Most North American Indians, women and men, played sports and games. Men played a game called "baggataway," at first as a religious rite. They used sticks and a ball, playing in teams of up to 500 warriors. Sometimes whole villages faced each other in bloody encounters that could last for days. Later, baggataway developed into lacrosse.

◁ A BAGGATAWAY player in full regalia. The stick had a hoop for catching and holding the ball.

▷ NORTH AMERICAN INDIANS played many winter games. They used sticks, balls, stones, and hoops, and there was also wrestling and tobogganing.

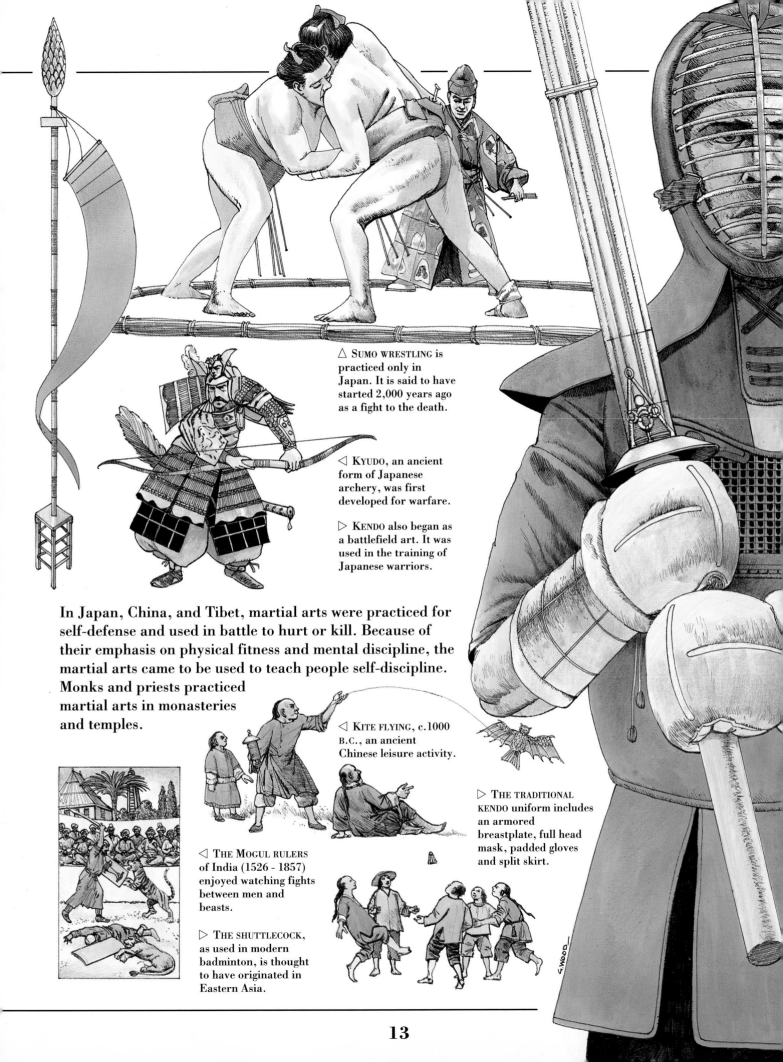

△ SUMO WRESTLING is practiced only in Japan. It is said to have started 2,000 years ago as a fight to the death.

◁ KYUDO, an ancient form of Japanese archery, was first developed for warfare.

▷ KENDO also began as a battlefield art. It was used in the training of Japanese warriors.

In Japan, China, and Tibet, martial arts were practiced for self-defense and used in battle to hurt or kill. Because of their emphasis on physical fitness and mental discipline, the martial arts came to be used to teach people self-discipline. Monks and priests practiced martial arts in monasteries and temples.

◁ KITE FLYING, c.1000 B.C., an ancient Chinese leisure activity.

▷ THE TRADITIONAL KENDO uniform includes an armored breastplate, full head mask, padded gloves and split skirt.

◁ THE MOGUL RULERS of India (1526 - 1857) enjoyed watching fights between men and beasts.

▷ THE SHUTTLECOCK, as used in modern badminton, is thought to have originated in Eastern Asia.

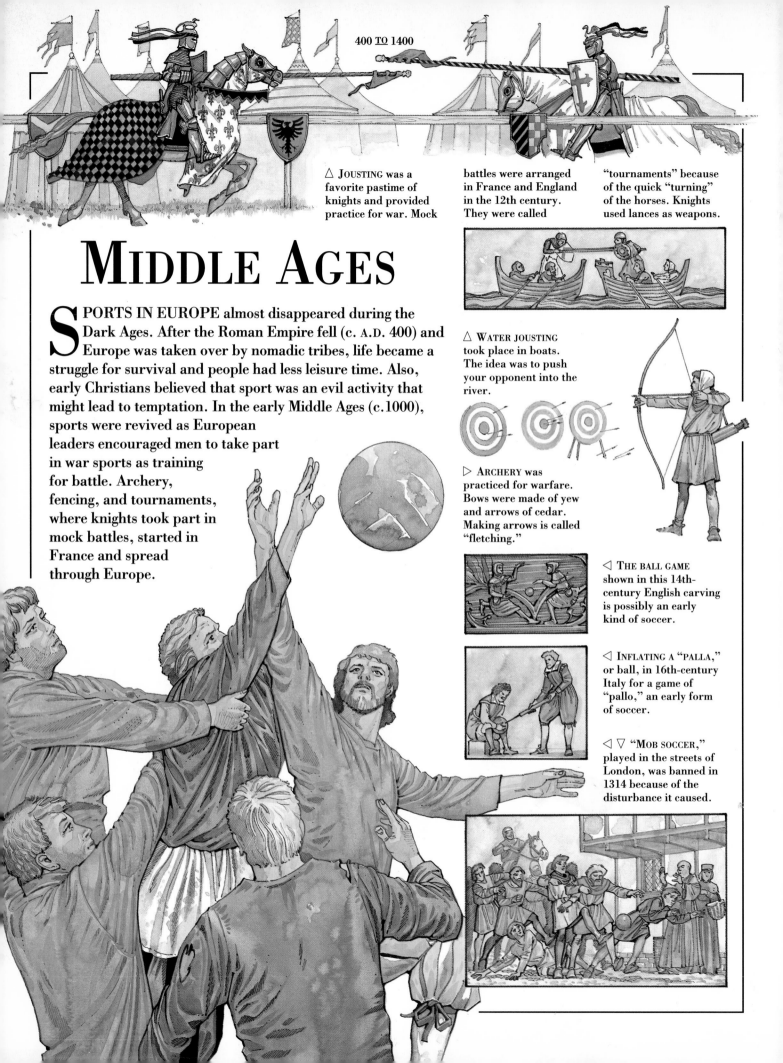

△ JOUSTING was a favorite pastime of knights and provided practice for war. Mock battles were arranged in France and England in the 12th century. They were called "tournaments" because of the quick "turning" of the horses. Knights used lances as weapons.

MIDDLE AGES

SPORTS IN EUROPE almost disappeared during the Dark Ages. After the Roman Empire fell (c. A.D. 400) and Europe was taken over by nomadic tribes, life became a struggle for survival and people had less leisure time. Also, early Christians believed that sport was an evil activity that might lead to temptation. In the early Middle Ages (c.1000), sports were revived as European leaders encouraged men to take part in war sports as training for battle. Archery, fencing, and tournaments, where knights took part in mock battles, started in France and spread through Europe.

△ WATER JOUSTING took place in boats. The idea was to push your opponent into the river.

▷ ARCHERY was practiced for warfare. Bows were made of yew and arrows of cedar. Making arrows is called "fletching."

◁ THE BALL GAME shown in this 14th-century English carving is possibly an early kind of soccer.

◁ INFLATING A "PALLA," or ball, in 16th-century Italy for a game of "pallo," an early form of soccer.

◁ ▽ "MOB SOCCER," played in the streets of London, was banned in 1314 because of the disturbance it caused.

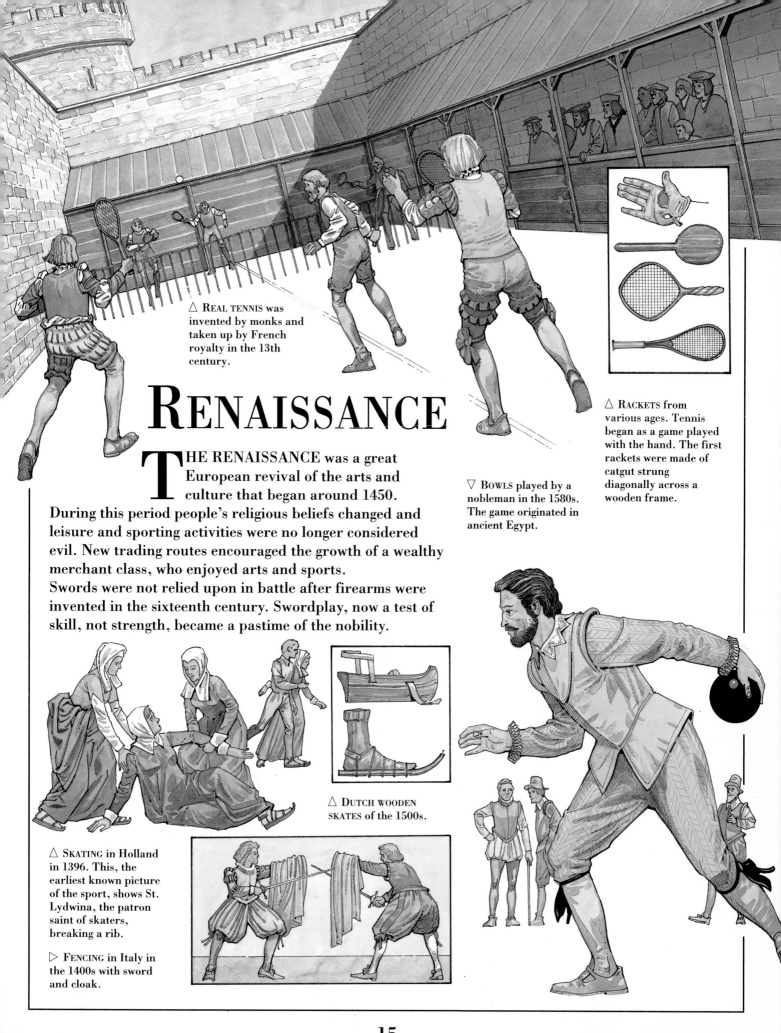

△ REAL TENNIS was invented by monks and taken up by French royalty in the 13th century.

RENAISSANCE

THE RENAISSANCE was a great European revival of the arts and culture that began around 1450. During this period people's religious beliefs changed and leisure and sporting activities were no longer considered evil. New trading routes encouraged the growth of a wealthy merchant class, who enjoyed arts and sports.

Swords were not relied upon in battle after firearms were invented in the sixteenth century. Swordplay, now a test of skill, not strength, became a pastime of the nobility.

△ RACKETS from various ages. Tennis began as a game played with the hand. The first rackets were made of catgut strung diagonally across a wooden frame.

▽ BOWLS played by a nobleman in the 1580s. The game originated in ancient Egypt.

△ DUTCH WOODEN SKATES of the 1500s.

△ SKATING in Holland in 1396. This, the earliest known picture of the sport, shows St. Lydwina, the patron saint of skaters, breaking a rib.

▷ FENCING in Italy in the 1400s with sword and cloak.

MODERN SPORTS

△ A DUTCH TILE shows a game like golf being played.

THE SEEDS OF MANY OF TODAY'S SPORTS were sown in the seventeenth and eighteenth centuries in Europe, and especially in Britain. The Puritan movement, which regarded sports as sinful, was growing in power in the early seventeenth century. To counteract this, King James I of England, an avid sportsman himself, issued a document in 1618 called *The Book of Sports*, stating that people may pursue "lawful recreations" on Sundays and holidays. Cricket, golf, rowing, billiards, tennis, and other racket games began to flourish. Soccer, a violent game with few rules, was a popular sport among village men. Wealthy people continued to enjoy hunting and shooting.

△ PELL-MELL, a game that originated around 1660 in France, involved hitting a ball through a ring.

△ BILLIARDS was probably first played in English and French coffeehouses.

▽ BILLIARD CUES were curved in the 17th century.

△ KOLVEN, as played in 17th-century Holland, was more like modern golf, but the Scots added the hole.

△ THE WORD "GOLF" originally meant club, from the Dutch word "kolf."

△ THE FIRST GOLF BALLS, or "featheries," were made in Scotland in c.1450 by stuffing a hatful of boiled goose feathers into a leather casing.

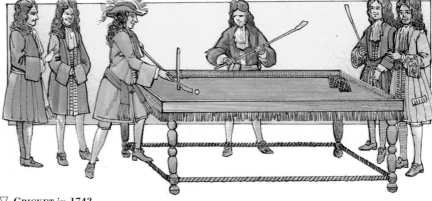

▽ CRICKET in 1743. The wicket consisted of two sticks and a twig and the bats were curved clubs.

△ ROWING, practiced for thousands of years, first became a leisure activity in 18th-century England.

△ DOGGETT'S COAT AND BADGE, given to the winner of a race between Thames boatmen.

◁ SKI RACING was practiced by the Lapps in the 18th century. They picked up objects as they skied.

▷ ARCHERY, which had virtually died out when the bow no longer had a military use, was revived as a sport in 1781 in England.

△ EARLY BASEBALL, played in the 18th century, was a combination of cricket and the game rounders.

Puritan influence had diminished by the late seventeenth century, and gambling, on everything from cockfighting to boxing, became a well organized business. In villages, blood sports like bullbaiting and bull running were popular. But the industrial revolution, which began around 1750, soon dramatically changed life for most ordinary Europeans. Cooped up in factories six days a week and living in squalid conditions, workers, including women and children, had little time and strength left to play games. Sports became a pastime of the nobility.

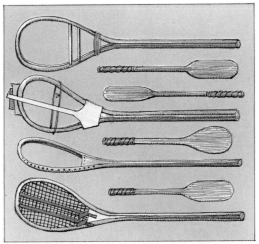

△ IN THE 18TH CENTURY, different versions of tennis and other racket sports became popular.

▷ PRIZEFIGHTING in England in 1788. Much money was involved in betting and prizes, and huge crowds came to watch matches.

ANIMALS

△ COCKFIGHTING became a popular betting sport in medieval England.

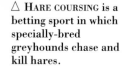

△ HARE COURSING is a betting sport in which specially-bred greyhounds chase and kill hares.

HUMANS HAVE USED ANIMALS in sports for thousands of years. Early humans proved their athletic skills by hunting and killing beasts. The hunt was a religious and sporting ritual that probably involved practice and competition. In ancient Egyptian times, hunting became a sport of the nobility and has remained so through the ages, first with spear and bow and arrow, and later with the gun.

Chasing and killing animals for fun is no longer regarded as "sport" by most people and movements have grown up to eradicate so-called "blood sports." But such activities as bullfighting, cockfighting, and fox hunting are still practiced and some seem to be growing in popularity. Animal charities in the Unitied States, for example, have reported a resurgence in dogfighting using pit bull terriers.

△ A POLO MATCH in London in 1873. An ancient game, polo was rediscovered by the English in India in the 1850s.

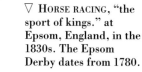

△ THE FIRST GRAND NATIONAL was run at Aintree in 1839. Steeplechasing began when the fencing of farmland was allowed.

▽ FOX HUNTING is practiced in Europe and the United States. Drag hunting has become popular in many places. Instead of chasing and killing a fox, the dogs chase an artificial scent that has been dragged over the hunt area.

▽ HORSE RACING, "the sport of kings." at Epsom, England, in the 1830s. The Epsom Derby dates from 1780.

18

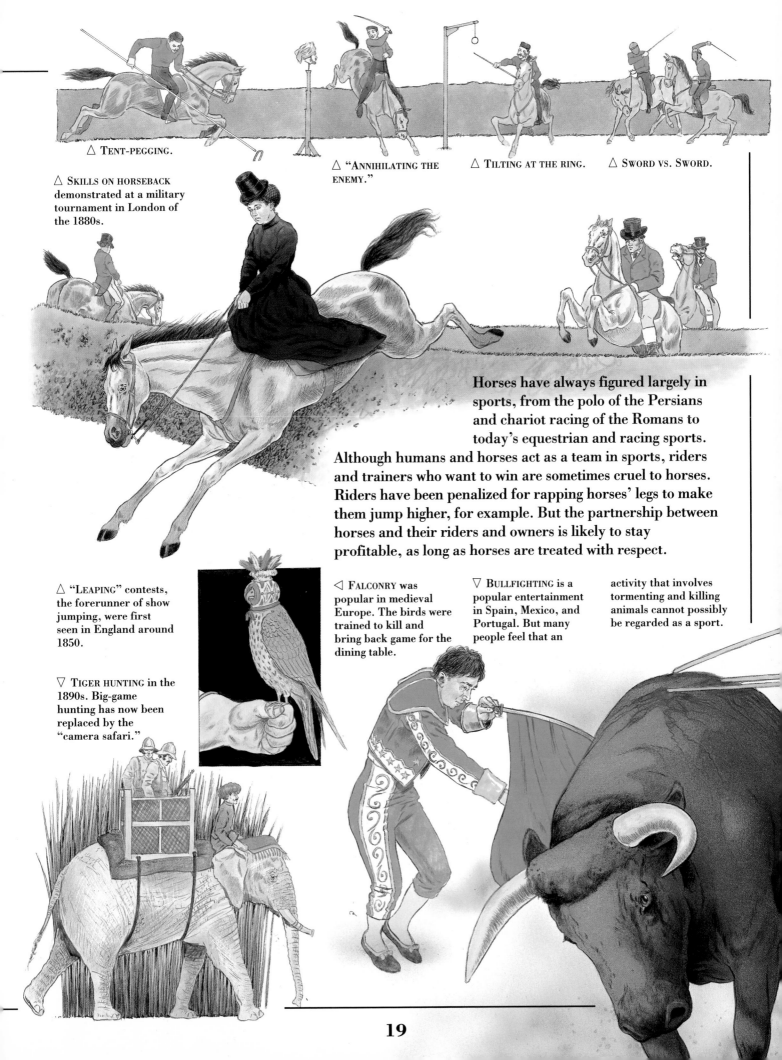

△ TENT-PEGGING.

△ "ANNIHILATING THE ENEMY."

△ TILTING AT THE RING.

△ SWORD VS. SWORD.

△ SKILLS ON HORSEBACK demonstrated at a military tournament in London of the 1880s.

Horses have always figured largely in sports, from the polo of the Persians and chariot racing of the Romans to today's equestrian and racing sports. Although humans and horses act as a team in sports, riders and trainers who want to win are sometimes cruel to horses. Riders have been penalized for rapping horses' legs to make them jump higher, for example. But the partnership between horses and their riders and owners is likely to stay profitable, as long as horses are treated with respect.

△ "LEAPING" contests, the forerunner of show jumping, were first seen in England around 1850.

▽ TIGER HUNTING in the 1890s. Big-game hunting has now been replaced by the "camera safari."

◁ FALCONRY was popular in medieval Europe. The birds were trained to kill and bring back game for the dining table.

▽ BULLFIGHTING is a popular entertainment in Spain, Mexico, and Portugal. But many people feel that an activity that involves tormenting and killing animals cannot possibly be regarded as a sport.

TEAM SPORTS

▽ RUGBY developed as a handling game. It was born at Rugby School, when a boy picked up the ball and ran with it instead of kicking it.

TEAM SPORTS had few rules at first. Physical contact sports such as soccer, played by peasants and laborers, were bloody affairs that caused injury and death. Eventually, with easier travel on the new railroads, games spread and competitions were arranged, and so rules were needed.

English universities, boarding schools, and military services, which had boys and men to keep occupied, were the first to organize team sports. In 1823, rugby was born at Rugby School. In 1848, Cambridge University set the first rules of soccer.

△ SOCCER at Rugby School in England in the mid-1800s, when it was first organized.

◁ THE FIRST inter-collegiate football game was played between Princeton and Rutgers on November 6, 1869.

△ THE ETON WALL GAME, a type of soccer played only at Eton, an English private school.

▽ CAPS WERE AWARDED in some sports to players when they represented their countries.

△ AUSTRALIAN RULES FOOTBALL developed in the mid-1800s as a mixture of rugby and soccer, an Irish form of the game.

◁ HEADING THE BALL is a technique only used in soccer.

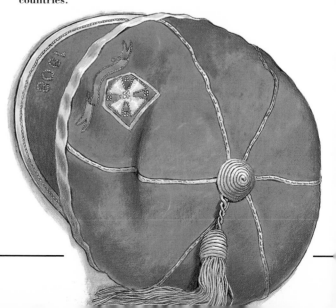

△ CRICKET at the Oval, in London, 19th century.

▷ LORD HAWKE (1860-1938), an English aristocrat, promoted international cricket and helped to modernize the game.

△ THE FIRST "TEST" (cricket international) in England took place against Australia at the Oval in 1880.

Team sports such as cricket, soccer, and hockey were spread by missionaries, the military, and traders throughout the British Empire, which, by the end of the nineteenth century, covered a quarter of the earth's land mass. British officers running the colonies had much leisure time in which to play and hold sports competitions. In India, they rediscovered the ancient game of polo, and exported it back to Britain.

The United States developed its own team sports at this time, including football, baseball, and volleyball.

▽ WOMEN PLAYED HOCKEY in long skirts, stockings, and blouses with ties.

△ ENGLISH WOMEN CRICKETERS of the 1890s. Women had been playing cricket since the early 1800s.

▽ BASEBALL took root in the United States in the early 1800s.

△ BASEBALL in England, 1874. It never caught on in England.

△ BASKETBALL was invented in 1891 in Springfield, Massachusetts by YMCA coach Dr. James Naismith.

GATHERINGS

▽ ▷ GYMNASTICS was revived in 1811 with the opening of the first open-air gym in Germany.

THE GREAT SPORTING EVENT at the end of the nineteenth century was the first modern Olympic Games. Inspired by the excavation of the original Olympic site in Greece (1875-81) and by the ancient aim to create goodwill, Baron Pierre de Coubertin, a French scholar, revived the Games. He was dismayed by what he saw as physical and moral decline in his own country, and believed that sports could help to reverse this trend. De Coubertin believed that the greatness of ancient Greece had been due to the high value placed on physical perfection and that sports played a large part in achieving physical fitness.

◁ TOSSING THE CABER at the Highland Games, which were revived from an ancient gathering.

It is said that De Coubertin had also been influenced by a visit to Rugby School in England, where he was impressed by the importance given to sports and morality. He may also have seen sports gatherings such as the Highland Games in Scotland and the Grasmere Games in the Lake District.

▷ THE LAWN TENNIS COURT, patented in Britain in 1874 and called "sphairistike." "Sphaira" is the Greek word for ball.

▽ RACKET PLAYERS play against a wall.

◁ ETON "FIVES" in the late 1800s. Racket sports and versions of fives, or handball, abounded.

▷ WIMBLEDON in the 1880s. By then the game was called lawn tennis, with a court and rules like today's.

▽ BADMINTON, adapted from the Indian game poona, and battledore and shuttlecock.

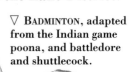

△ THE 800 METERS RACE. Women competed for the first time in the Olympics in 1928.

▷ A FELL (HILL) RACE at Grasmere, England, in 1901, part of a traditional sports festival still held today.

◁ RAY EWRY (U.S.) won 10 Olympic gold medals in standing jump events (1900-08), which are no longer held.

The first modern Olympics were held in Athens as a tribute to the Games' ancient Greek origins. Although only twelve countries took part, the games were considered a success and the movement took off. Apart from during the world wars, the Olympic Games have been held every four years since 1896.

In the late nineteenth century lawn tennis was invented and organized in England. The All England Lawn Tennis Championship (Wimbledon) was first held in 1877 and the U.S. championship in 1881.

Athens, 1896

▷ OLYMPIC MEDALS.

Antwerp, 1920

Amsterdam, 1928

△ THE OLYMPIC STADIUM at Athens in 1896, when crowds of 80,000 turned up to watch the games.

▷ THE START of the 1896 Olympic 100 meters race, one of 12 athletic events.

MAKING RULES

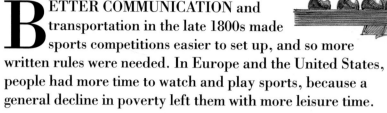

BETTER COMMUNICATION and transportation in the late 1800s made sports competitions easier to set up, and so more written rules were needed. In Europe and the United States, people had more time to watch and play sports, because a general decline in poverty left them with more leisure time.

△ NINEPINS, a game in which the number of pins was set by religious reformer Martin Luther in the 1500s.

◁ FENCING was included in the first modern Olympics in 1896.

△ TENPIN BOWLING in the U.S. in the 1870s. Ninepins, which had been taken over by criminals, was banned, so a pin was added.

◁ DUELING WITH SWORDS in the 1870s. Strict rules applied to duels, which had been common for centuries as a way of settling disputes. Dueling later developed into the sport of fencing.

Boxing was transformed by a new set of rules. Fighting with the bare fist had been a vicious sport since ancient Greek times. It was no better in nineteenth-century England, when prizefighters fought until one was beaten badly or dropped from exhaustion. In 1865, the Marquess of Queensberry drew up twelve rules that, with only minor changes, have been followed worldwide ever since.

▽ U.S. WORLD HEAVYWEIGHT CHAMPION Jack Johnson was knocked out in the 26th round by Jess Willard in 1915. Boxing under the Queensberry rules required padded gloves, a canvas floor, and 3-minute rounds.

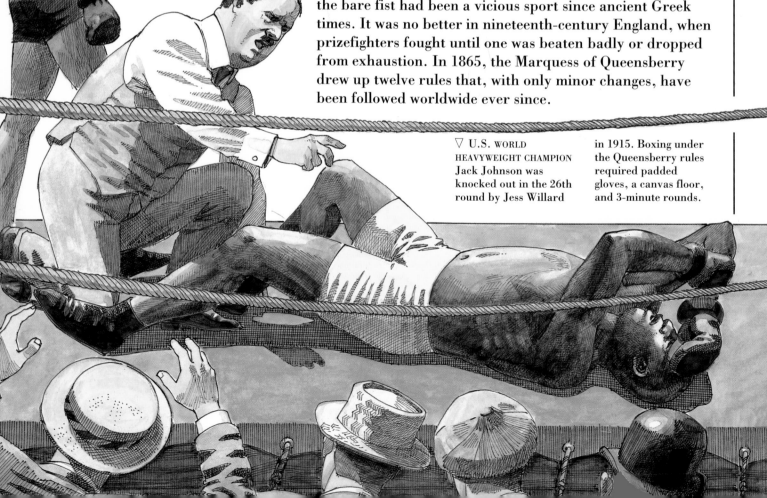

WHEELS

△ EARLY BICYCLES – high-wheeler (1), 3-wheeler (2), tandem (3).

◁ MOTORCYCLE RACING in the 1920s. The basic design of these machines has changed little over the years.

▽ THIS FRENCH RACING MACHINE of 1903 was built for speed.

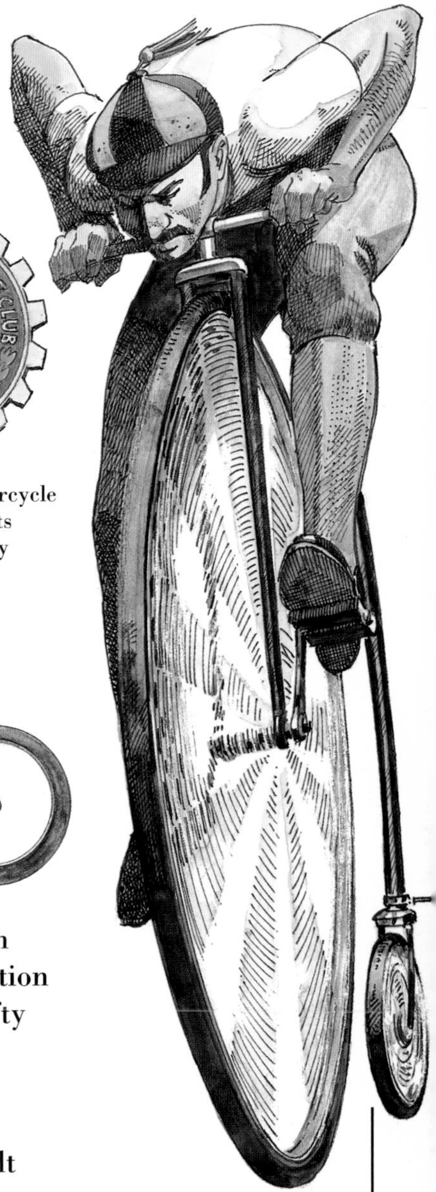

△ CLUBS for motorcycle and car enthusiasts started in the early 1900s.

△ BICYCLE RACING in 1875 on a high-wheeler, also known as a "penny-farthing."

SPORTS ON WHEELS began with chariot racing. It later flourished with the development of the bicycle and the invention of the internal-combustion engine in 1862. Bicycling, initially without pedals, had been going for fifty years before the first race, in Paris in 1868. But soon after the arrival of the motorcycle and automobile in the 1880s, racing began in earnest.

The first organized car race took place on the roads of France in 1895. As machines became faster, racing was moved from the roads to specially-built circuits. The first Indianapolis 500 race was held in 1911.

△ RACING at Brooklands, England, in 1909. Brooklands was the first banked car racing track.

Peugeot

BUGATTI

WATER SPORTS

RELICS FROM ANCIENT EGYPT show people swimming, and rowing and swimming were features of daily life in ancient Greece. The Greeks had no interest in swimming as a sport, however, but rowing contests go back at least 2,500 years.

Formal swimming competitions originated in Japan in 1603, but swimming was not taken up in Europe until the nineteenth century because it was believed that water spread disease. Swimming was included in the 1896 Athens Olympics. Sailing was the chief means of water transport for thousands of years before it developed as a sport in England in the late sixteenth century.

▷ DIVING in the 1932 Olympics. Contestants were (and still are) judged on style, technique, and difficulty.

△ MATTHEW WEBB was the first to swim the English channel in 1875. It took him 21 hours, 45 minutes.

△ SWIMMERS dive in at the start of the women's 400 meters race at the 1932 Olympic Games.

△ SAILING, or yacht racing, in 1851, when the New York yacht America won a race around the Isle of Wight, England.

This led to the founding of the America's Cup, still raced for between countries.

▽ The modern kayak developed from the Inuit kayak. Canoeing as a sport first became popular in the 1860s.

▷ ROWING (one oar) and sculling (two) were revolutionized by the invention of the outrigger and the sliding seat.

Sliding seat

Inuit kayak

Outrigger

◁ THE UNIVERSITY BOAT RACE in 1878, an annual fixture between rowers of Oxford and Cambridge since 1829.

△ HENLEY, England in the 1900s. The Henley Regatta has been held annually since 1839.

WINNING WOMEN

U NTIL RECENTLY, women have found their progress hindered in all but a few sports because of prejudice and mistaken notions of femininity. Women were banned from even watching the ancient Greek Olympics, and were not allowed to compete in the first modern Olympics in 1896. But despite the obstacles, a few women in the late nineteenth and early twentieth centuries became sporting legends. One was U.S. swimmer Gertrude Ederle, who knocked two hours off the men's record when swimming the English channel in 1926.

Rarely do women compete with men, but they have produced world champions in equestrian sports and car racing and provided coxes for men's rowing crews. In the 1980s, U.S. drag racer Shirley Muldowney became the only person to win three world titles in the sport.

△ WOMEN were allowed to compete at Wimbledon in 1884, seven years after the competition began. The U.S. Championships opened in 1881, and women were invited to compete in 1887. Tennis was the first Olympic sport for women, included in the 1900 Paris Olympics.

Sonja Henie

Suzanne Lenglen

Gertrude Ederle.

Lottie Dod

"Babe" Didrikson

△ LOTTIE DOD (U.K.), at 15 the youngest Wimbledon champion (1887), played golf and hockey for England.

△ FRENCH TENNIS STAR Suzanne Lenglen's play and personality tranformed tennis in the 1920s.

△ "BABE" DIDRIKSON (U.S.) won 1932 Olympic javelin and hurdles golds and became a champion golfer.

△ SONJA HENIE (Norway) won 10 world skating titles (1927-36) and 3 Olympic golds before becoming a film star in Hollywood.

△ GERTRUDE EDERLE (U.S.) was the first woman to swim the English channel (1926). She beat the men's record by 2 hours.

HEROES

△ YANKEE STADIUM, built in 1923. Logo of the New York Yankees (below), team of baseball hero Babe Ruth.

THE 1920s saw a dramatic change in sports. Before that, sports, with a few exceptions, were regarded as a pastime and played largely by amateurs, or people who were not paid. But with the advent of live radio broadcasts of games, sports grew into mass entertainment, especially in the United States, where advertisers seized upon sports as a vehicle to popularize their goods. Sports became big business, and sports heroes became living legends. The best sports figures were paid to play full time, and became professional players. Some sports, such as tennis and track and field, remained games for amateurs only.

▽ TENNIS STAR Bill Tilden (U.S.), unbeaten for 6 years (1920-25) in major competitions.

Bill Tilden

▽ PAAVO NURMI (Finland), the "Flying Finn," won 9 Olympic gold medals in the 1920s.

▽ WALTER HAGEN (U.S.) improved the standing of professional golfers in the 1920s. In the 1930s, amateur Bobby Jones (U.S., inset) was the first golfing idol.

◁ U.S. SWIMMER Johnny Weissmuller won 5 Olympic golds in 1924 and 1928.

▽ JACK DEMPSEY (U.S.), world heavyweight boxing champion for 7 years (1919-26).

△ GENE TUNNEY (U.S.) won the world title from Jack Dempsey and later retired undefeated.

▽ BABE RUTH, perhaps the most famous of American sports heroes, was one of baseball's biggest hitters ever.

Paavo Nurmi.

Bobby Jones.

Johnny Weissmuller.

Walter Hagen.

Jack Dempsey.

Babe Ruth.

Harold Larwood.

Don Bradman.

△ CRICKET FAST BOWLER Larwood headed England's 1932-33 "bodyline" tour of Australia, to curb the run-making of Bradman.

△ THE JULES RIMET TROPHY, for soccer's World Cup, named after the Frenchman who pioneered the competition.

WORLD STAGE

◁ JESSE OWENS (U.S.) won 4 gold medals in sprints and long jump at the Berlin Olympics, a blow to the Nazi ideal of white superiority.

▷ URUGUAY, the hosts, beat Argentina 4-2 in the first World Cup final, in 1930.

▽ THE OLYMPIC TORCH was first relayed from Greece at the start of the 1936 Games.

POLITICS AND SPORTS became intertwined in the 1930s, as political leaders began to use sports to popularize their governments, a trend that has lasted until today. Benito Mussolini, the fascist dictator of Italy, poured money into Italy's soccer team, helping them to win the World Cup in 1934 and 1938. The German Nazi leader Adolf Hitler put on a lavish Olympic Games in Berlin in 1936 to try to convince the world of the success of his anti-Jewish and antiblack regime. Nine years later, at the end of World War II, the world learned of the true horrors of the Nazi regime.

BERLIN 1936
1 16 AUG.
OLYMPISCHE SPIELE

WAR AND PEACE

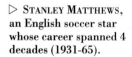

△ THE FIRST BLACK PLAYER in major league baseball. Jackie Robinson (1947, above left), and in football, Kenny Washington (1946, below).

WORLD WAR II (1939-45) brought international sports to a virtual standstill. Just before that, Americans marveled at the feats of Joe Louis, world heavyweight boxer. Although black men and women found that sports provided opportunities denied to them in other aspects of life, they still found their progress hindered in team sports. It was not until 1946 that the United States saw its first black professional football player, Kenny Washington, and in 1947, its first black baseball player, Jackie Robinson. But both men were still subjected to racial abuse, some from their teammates.

Sport flourished after the war. The Soviet Union brought its athletes out from behind the "Iron Curtain" and they made an immediate impact on international sports.

△ BRITISH CRICKETER Denis Compton was one of the first sportsmen outside the United States to appear in advertisements.

◁ JOE LOUIS downs a contender. His long reign as world heavyweight boxing champion (1937-49) helped black athletes to be accepted as professionals throughout the country.

▽ ROGER BANNISTER (U.K.) ran the first 4-minute mile in 1954, breaking a world record that had stood since 1945.

▷ STANLEY MATTHEWS, an English soccer star whose career spanned 4 decades (1931-65).

▽ GYMNAST LARISSA LAYYNINA was one of many Soviet athletes to gain Olympic success in 1956.

▷ MOSCOW DYNAMO made a brief tour of the U.K. in 1945 before Soviet soccer disappeared from the international scene for several years.

POWER GAMES

FROM THE EARLY 1950s, television became a force in determining how sports should be played. In the United States, football was tailored to the requirements of the TV networks, which, for example, insisted the game be divided into four quarters to allow for advertisements during the intervals. Television brought sports to a wider audience; by 1956, three quarters of American households had TV sets. Sportsmen and women from all over the world became TV stars, and international competitions flourished because they could now be seen at home.

△ LIVE TELEVISION coverage of an exciting football game in 1958 revived the sport.

△ NATIONAL TENSIONS were played out between Hungary and the Soviet Union in the 1956 Olympic water polo semi-final. A month earlier, the Soviet Union had invaded Hungary and over 7,000 hungarians had died. The referee ended the match after blood was shed, with Hungary leading 4-0.

▽ THE "BLACK POWER" SALUTE was given by some U.S. athletes on the winners' rostrum during the 1968 Olympics, to protest against racism in America. They were sent home for their actions.

◁ ROD LAVER (Australia) won the Wimbledon men's title in 1968, the year it was opened to professionals, to become the first professional champion.

△ ETHIOPIAN ABEBE BIKILA, barefoot winner of the 1960 Olympic marathon, encouraged Africans in sports.

◁ SOCCER STARS Pelé (Brazil) and Bobby Moore (England) exchange shirts after the 1970 World Cup.

◁ WHEN THE CRICKETER Basil D'Oliveira (left) was selected for England's 1968 tour abroad, South Africa objected because he was black. South Africa was later banished from international sports because of its apartheid regime, in which the majority non-white population was denied many rights and was forced to live separately from white people.

THE OLYMPICS

The magnificent Munich Olympic Stadium (shown here) provided a backdrop for what promised to be a memorable Games in 1972. But Palestinian terrorists caused the deaths of eleven members of the Israeli team, and this heralded a period of Olympic history overshadowed by terrorism and politics. The Olympics had become the target for any group or government wanting to hold it for ransom.

◁ OLYMPIC GOLD MEDAL of 1972 – achievements such as U.S. swimmer Mark Spitz's 7 golds were overshadowed by the act of terrorism.

◁ A TERRORIST appears outside the Israeli quarters in 1972, where team members were being held for ransom.

▽ GYMNAST Nadia Comaneci (Romania) received the first perfect score in 1976.

▽ BORIS ONISHCHENKO (U.S.S.R.) was disqualified from the 1976 Olympics for cheating in the modern pentathlon.

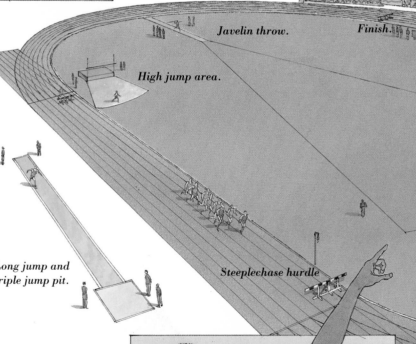

Javelin throw.

Finish.

High jump area.

Long jump and triple jump pit.

Steeplechase hurdle

▽ SEB COE (U.K., right) beats compatriot Steve Ovett, the 800 m gold medalist, who took third place in the 1980 Olympic 1500 m race. Coe went on to retain his title in 1984.

▷ BRITISH DECATHLETE Daley Thompson, gold-medalist in 1980 and 1984, and U.S. sprinter and long jumper Carl Lewis (right), who won 7 gold medals between 1984 and 1992.

After the Munich Games, each of the next three Games saw at least one major sporting power withdraw. In Montreal in 1976, a black boycott, in protest over New Zealand's sporting links with South Africa, led to the withdrawal of 32 countries. In 1980, the United States and other countries boycotted the Moscow Olympics after the Soviet Union invaded Afghanistan. The Soviet Union and its allies retaliated in 1984 by withdrawing from the Los Angeles Games.

Although the Olympics were strictly for amateurs, manufacturers were paying some Olympic athletes to use their equipment. It is now known that communist bloc governments paid their athletes to practice full time. In the United States, top athletes received paid scholarships to universities. In 1981, the International Olympic Committee began to allow athletes to keep sponsorship and prize money for their expenses and retirement, though they are still not paid for competing.

△ THE STARTING PISTOL is part of an electronic system that includes a photo finish and times races to 1/100th second.

△ STARTING BLOCKS are used by runners in the sprints.

△ RUNNING SHOES are worth a great deal of money to top athletes sponsored by their manufacturers.

△ THE OLYMPIC FLAME (first appeared 1928) symbolizes the athletes' aim for perfection.

Shot-put circle.

Pole vault.

Steeplechase water jump.

Hammer and discus circle.

Running lanes.

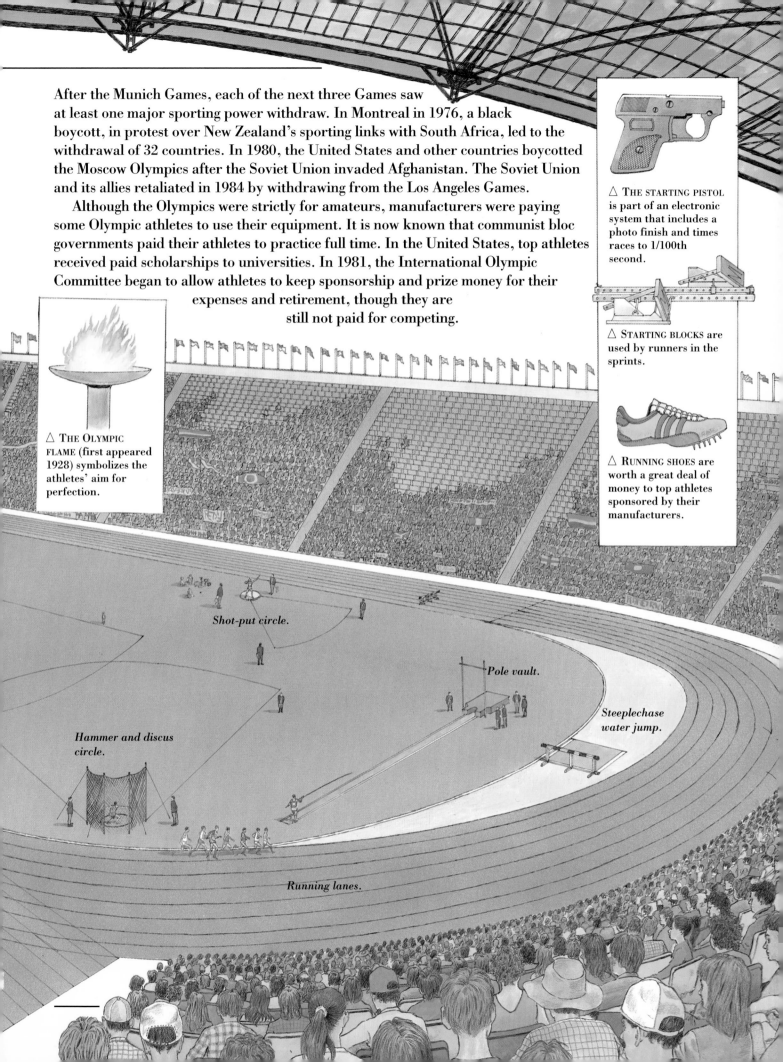

WINTER SPORTS

SKIING AND SKATING have been human activities since ancient times as means of transportation on snow and ice. Skating as a leisure activity dates from fourteenth-century Holland, when races were held on the canals.

Winter sports first appeared on the Olympic stage when figure skating was included in the 1908 program in London. It appeared again in 1920, along with ice hockey.

The first separate Winter Olympics were held in 1924, at Chamonix, in France. It was decided in 1992 to hold the next winter Games in 1994 and every four years thereafter, instead of in the same year as the summer Olympics.

△ A STATUE of Sonja Henie (Norway), the Olympic skater who later made movies.

△ SKATING on a frozen lake in New York's Central Park in the 1860s.

◁ SPEED SKATING was popular in the early 1900s. Men's world championships have been held since 1889.

▷ A HURDLE RACE in snowshoes in Canada in the early 1900s, when trappers, miners and loggers took part.

△ U.S. SPEED SKATER Eric Heiden won all 5 men's gold medals in speed skating at the 1980 Winter Olympics.

△ SKI-JUMPING from great heights originated in Norway in the 1860. It calls for courage as well as skill and grace.

△ TORVILL AND DEAN achieved a perfect 6.0 score across the board at the 1984 Winter Olympics in Sarajevo.

◁ BIATHLON, A combination of cross-country skiing and shooting at targets, has military origins.

△ ALPINE SKIING was pioneered by the British, who devised slalom and downhill events.

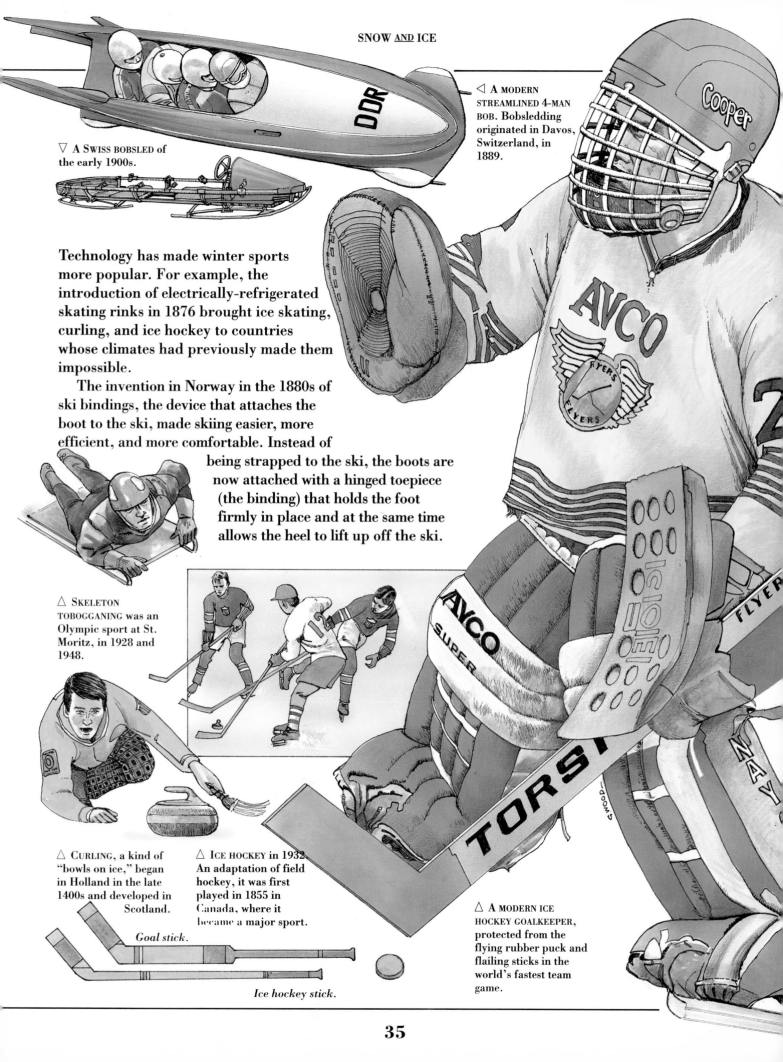

△ A MODERN STREAMLINED 4-MAN BOB. Bobsledding originated in Davos, Switzerland, in 1889.

▽ A SWISS BOBSLED of the early 1900s.

Technology has made winter sports more popular. For example, the introduction of electrically-refrigerated skating rinks in 1876 brought ice skating, curling, and ice hockey to countries whose climates had previously made them impossible.

The invention in Norway in the 1880s of ski bindings, the device that attaches the boot to the ski, made skiing easier, more efficient, and more comfortable. Instead of being strapped to the ski, the boots are now attached with a hinged toepiece (the binding) that holds the foot firmly in place and at the same time allows the heel to lift up off the ski.

△ SKELETON TOBOGGANING was an Olympic sport at St. Moritz, in 1928 and 1948.

△ CURLING, a kind of "bowls on ice," began in Holland in the late 1400s and developed in Scotland.

△ ICE HOCKEY in 1932. An adaptation of field hockey, it was first played in 1855 in Canada, where it became a major sport.

Goal stick.

Ice hockey stick.

△ A MODERN ICE HOCKEY GOALKEEPER, protected from the flying rubber puck and flailing sticks in the world's fastest team game.

MODERN AGE

SPORTS TODAY is a worldwide industry. Sports stars receive enormous sums of money to play in matches, to wear certain company logos on their clothes and to use certain brands of equipment. They have agents and managers to represent them and promote their interests, and some become millionaires while they are still teenagers. Television stations bid for the right to show matches and events, and companies pay a high price to advertise during the intervals to promote their brands.

The sports industry also caters to people in developed countries, who, as a result of shorter working hours and a higher standard of living in the twentieth century, have more leisure time than ever in which to enjoy sports. A huge industry has grown up around providing equipment and "leisure clothes" for them. Sports are now an important part of the economy of every developed country in the world.

△ TODAY'S GRAND PRIX racing car is like a 200 mph (300 km/h) speeding billboard displaying the names of the sport's sponsors.

▽ BICYCLE RACING also relies on sponsorship. The teams in the big touring races all represent sponsors.

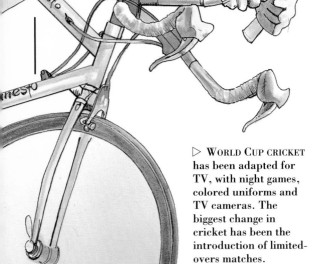

△ TENNIS STAR John McEnroe's tantrums on court in the 1980s earned him the nickname "Superbrat."

◁ ICE HOCKEY BRAWLS are common. Sending players to the penalty box, or "sin bin," doesn't seem to help.

▷ WORLD CUP CRICKET has been adapted for TV, with night games, colored uniforms and TV cameras. The biggest change in cricket has been the introduction of limited-overs matches.

Cricketer Chris Lewis.

△ SOCCER PLAYERS are required to take time off while they recover from injury.

◁ DISABLED PEOPLE have many opportunities to compete in sports. The Paralympics are held every four years, after the Olympic Games.

△ ELENA MOUKHINA, world champion Soviet gymnast in 1978, was put under too much physical strain and is now disabled.

▷ CANADIAN SPRINTER Ben Johnson lost his 1988 Olympic gold medal and world record when he tested positive for drugs.

▽ ARGENTINIAN SOCCER STAR Diego Maradona has admitted to taking drugs.

△ FOOTBALL PLAYERS usually have short careers (under 10 years) and some suffer permanent injuries.

The partnership of sports, money, and the media has not been a total success story. The lure of money has resulted in a win-at-all-costs attitude among individuals, teams and even nations. The use of drugs to enhance performance is now widespread. Poor sportmanship is also spreading. One notorious example is tennis star John McEnroe, whose behavior at Wimbledon in 1981 and after has been copied by other young players.

So much pressure is put on sportsmen and women, either by the rewards offered or by coaches whose job might depend on winning, that serious injuries and early retirement have become all too common.

Ben Johnson.

Diego Maradona.

SEOUL1988 159

▽ U.S. WORLD HEAVYWEIGHT champion boxer Mike Tyson has seen his career marred by scandal.

Mike Tyson.

*Cricket
(bowling)
100 mph
(160 km/h)*

*Baseball
(pitching)
101 mph
(162 km/h)*

SPEED

*Malcolm
Campbell.*

SPEED IS THE DRIVING FORCE behind many sports. To be the fastest must have motivated the earliest peoples to compete at sports. Some sports, such as sprinting and drag racing, depend almost totally on speed, but also require skill and tactics to produce and use that raw power.

Car racing is the fastest sport in the world, and it gets faster with each new advance in technology. Grand Prix race cars are now constructed using computer-aided design. The invention of the "monocoque" frame in the mid-1960s, the turbo-charged engine in 1979, and the use of carbon fiber material have all made Grand Prix cars lighter and faster.

△ IN JAI ALAI, said to be the fastest ball game, players fling the ball at speeds of up to 185 mph (300 km/h).

1 GLENN CURTISS'S BIKE used an aircraft engine to reach 135 mph (220 km/h) in 1907.

2 MALCOLM CAMPBELL was the first to reach 300 mph (483 km/h) on land, in 1935.

4 THE BELGIAN Camille Jenatzy in his electric car in 1899, the first vehicle to exceed 60 mph (100 km/h).

5 ICE YACHTS have made speeds of 140 mph (230 km/h) and from 1600 to 1830, were the fastest means of transportation at 50 mph (80 km/h).

6 GAR WOOD was the first to reach 100 mph (161 km/h) on water – in his powerboat *Miss America IX* in 1931.

7 MALCOLM CAMPBELL, in *Bluebird*, the name given to all his and son Donald's boats, held the WSR from 1937 to 1950.

8 DONALD CAMPBELL, the first to reach 200 mph (322 km/h) on water in 1955, set 7 WSRs but was killed in 1967 going 298 mph (480 km/h).

Table tennis
105 mph (170 km/h).

Tennis (serve)
140 mph (222 km/h).

Squash 145 mph
(232 km/h).

Golf 170 mph
(273 km/h).

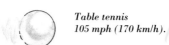
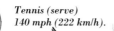
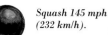

△ It is interesting to compare speeds in sports. Top female sprinters reach speeds of 20 mph (33 km/h), males 22 mph (36 km/h), whereas swimmers reach less than 6 mph (9 km/h). Roller skaters hit 27 mph (43 km/h) and water-skiers have exceeded 186 mph (300 km/h). Greyhounds have reached 40 mph (67 km/h), horses with jockeys nearly 45 mph (70 km/h), and racing pigeons, with the help of a following wind, as much as 110 mph (179 km/h).

There has been an official world land speed record (LSR) since 1898, and a water speed record (WSR) since 1928. Some men have held both – British racers Henry Segrave, Malcolm Campbell, and his son Donald. Segrave and Donald Campbell are among those who died in their machines.

3 GARY GABELICH was the first to hit 620 mph (1,000 km/h), in 1970 in his rocket-powered *Blue Flame*.

9 DONALD CAMPBELL, in *Proteus Bluebird*, was the first to reach 400 mph (644 km/h) on land, a record he set in 1964.

10 KEN WARBY set a water speed record of 318 mph (514 km/h) in his hydroplane *Spirit of Australia* in 1978.

11 GINA CAMPBELL, the daughter of Donald, continued the family tradition with a women's WSR of 123 mph (198 km/h) in 1985.

12 DON VESCO, on his 'streamliner' bike *Lightning Bolt*, set a world motorcycle speed record of 317.5 mph (512 km/h) in 1978.

13 RICHARD NOBLE set the official LSR of 632 mph (1,019 km/h) in his jet-powered, aluminum-wheeled car *Thrust 2* in 1983.

△ ▷ FOOTBALL UNIFORMS from the early 1900s. Numbers and, later, players' names, appeared on uniforms.

△ AS SOCCER has become a faster-moving game, the uniform has become briefer. During the 1870s (1) only the color of the cap distinguished the teams. Uniform jerseys arrived in the 1880s (2). By the 1930s (3) the stripe was lighter but the boots were still heavy.

DRESS AND EQUIPMENT

DRESS IN SPORTS is dictated by advances in technology and by fashion. The development of new fibers such as Lycra, invented in the 1970s, has revolutionized clothes in sports such as bicycling. Lycra helps material cling to the body, providing freedom of movement and causing little wind resistance. But participants in sports such as mountain climbing have found that technology cannot improve upon centuries-old materials like silk, which provides insulation from the cold as well as protection against the hot sun.

Sports clothes for women took a long time to appear. In the nineteenth century, when women began to participate in sports, it was believed that short skirts were indecent and thin clothing was impractical, so women were forced to wear unsuitable clothes for sports.

△ MODERN SOCCER wear is brief, with lightweight shoes. Shirts usually carry advertisers' logos.

▽ ALFA ROMEO, leading Grand Prix car of the late 1940s, with drivers like Juan Manuel Fangio of Argentina.

▷ A 1912 Peugeot, one of the earliest Grand Prix winners.

◁ A 1908 MERCEDES. It won the 1908 French Grand Prix despite 11 tire changes.

△ BENTLEYS dominated the Le Mans 24-hour race in the late 1920s, a tribute to their reliability.

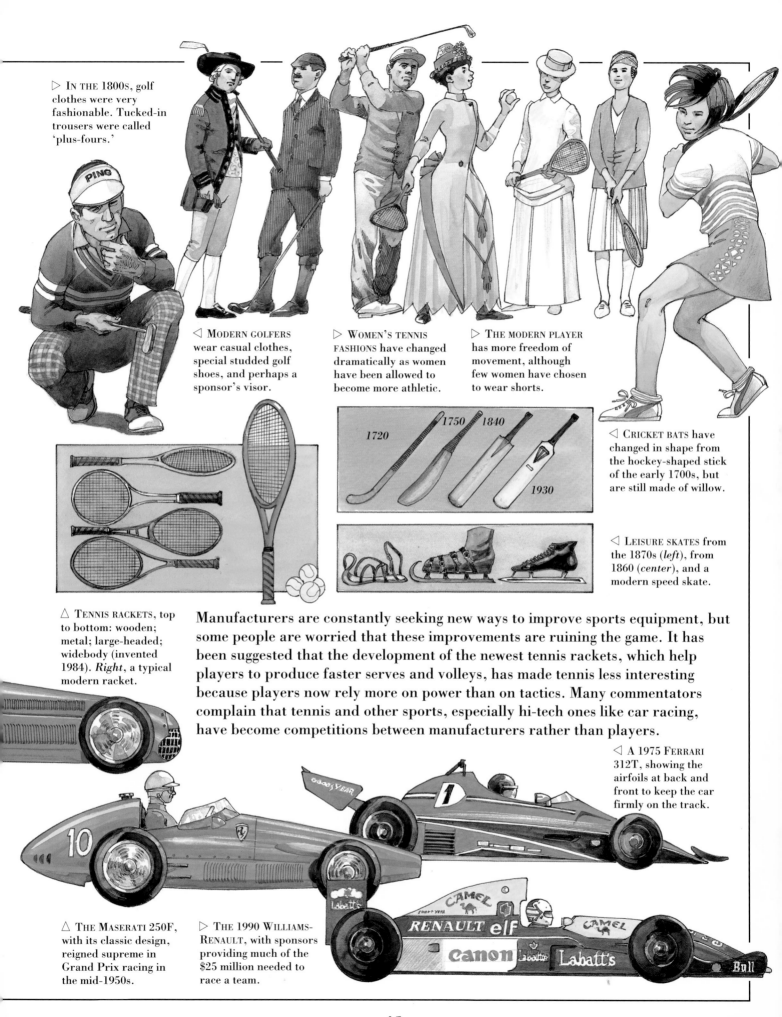

▷ IN THE 1800s, golf clothes were very fashionable. Tucked-in trousers were called 'plus-fours.'

◁ MODERN GOLFERS wear casual clothes, special studded golf shoes, and perhaps a sponsor's visor.

▷ WOMEN'S TENNIS FASHIONS have changed dramatically as women have been allowed to become more athletic.

▷ THE MODERN PLAYER has more freedom of movement, although few women have chosen to wear shorts.

1720 1750 1840 1930

◁ CRICKET BATS have changed in shape from the hockey-shaped stick of the early 1700s, but are still made of willow.

◁ LEISURE SKATES from the 1870s (*left*), from 1860 (*center*), and a modern speed skate.

△ TENNIS RACKETS, top to bottom: wooden; metal; large-headed; widebody (invented 1984). *Right*, a typical modern racket.

Manufacturers are constantly seeking new ways to improve sports equipment, but some people are worried that these improvements are ruining the game. It has been suggested that the development of the newest tennis rackets, which help players to produce faster serves and volleys, has made tennis less interesting because players now rely more on power than on tactics. Many commentators complain that tennis and other sports, especially hi-tech ones like car racing, have become competitions between manufacturers rather than players.

◁ A 1975 FERRARI 312T, showing the airfoils at back and front to keep the car firmly on the track.

△ THE MASERATI 250F, with its classic design, reigned supreme in Grand Prix racing in the mid-1950s.

▷ THE 1990 WILLIAMS-RENAULT, with sponsors providing much of the $25 million needed to race a team.

TECHNOLOGY

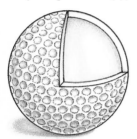

△ PEOPLE USE technology in order to improve their health. This equipment for medical gymnastics was invented in 1897. A weight lifting machine (1); an early sit-up machine (2), and a riding machine (3).

TECHNOLOGY IS USED IN SPORTS not only to help players go faster and improve their games, but to reduce the chances of injury. Safeguards are vital in sports such as car racing, where an accident at high speed can have horrific consequences. Tracks, cars, and driving suits are all designed to make the sport as safe as possible.

Protection is paramount, too, for participants in physical contact sports. Football players, for example, first wore leather flying helmets. Plastic helmets were introduced in 1939, and are now filled with special shock-absorbent foam with inflatable inner sections. Even in sports such as tennis, equipment is designed to prevent muscular damage.

◁ GOLF BALLS are constructed for distance, accuracy, and control. The dimples in their surface are essential for good, consistent flight.

▷ IMPROVED MATERIALS have made tennis rackets more powerful. At the same time, manufacturers have built-in features to reduce shock injuries to arm and shoulder.

▷ THE DUNLOP *REVELATION* racket uses carbon rods encased in a shock-absorbent material.

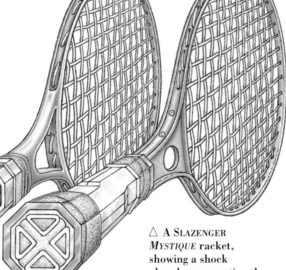

▽ THE RACING OUTFIT worn by Formula One racing drivers.

Fire-resistant fiberglass helmet with impact-absorbing foam inside.

Unbreakable fire-resistant visor.

Emergency air system in helmet, activated by push-button in case of fire.

Strong epaulettes allow driver to be hauled to safety in an emergency.

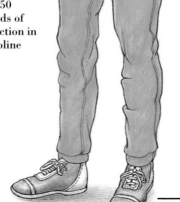

△ A SLAZENGER *MYSTIQUE* racket, showing a shock absorber separating the handle elements.

3. The partially-molded frame shows how the thermoplastic fits over the metal core underneath.

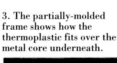

Flame-resistant outer coverall gives 50 seconds of protection in a gasoline fire.

1. This hi-tech injection-molded Dunlop tennis racket is made by first constructing a metal core.

2. The core is fitted into the racket mold and the inner material, a thermoplastic, is injected in.

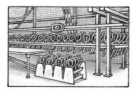

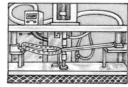

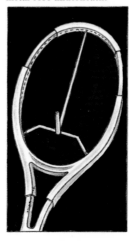

4. The mold is removed and the racket is heated, causing the metal core to melt and run out, leaving the frame hollow.

5. Quality-controlled machinery checks the racket for stiffness. Hi-tech rackets like this one are strong and light.

THE FUTURE

▷ NEW GAMES are competitive, but put the interests of the players first, which is a hopeful trend for the future. Earthball is one such game in which taking part and having fun are more important than the result.

▷ IN EARTHBALL, the idea is to handle the huge ball over the other side's goal line. Teams and time of play are unlimited, and the goal lines are about 650 feet (200 m) apart.

TELEVISION, ADVERTISING, new technology, and politics all affect sports. Like many other activities in today's high-technology world, sports are changing more rapidly than ever before.

As industrialized societies seem to be growing more violent, some people worry that there may be a return to gladiator sports, similar to those Roman times, in which the participants play to kill in order to entertain a bloodthirsty public.

Many people want to see sports freed from competition and from the control of big business, so that the joy of sports comes simply from taking part. "New games," developed in the United States, such as Earthball (*shown here*), have been designed to bring people together to play sports just for fun.

The sports of the future might be played inside your head. The latest in computer game advances, called "virtual reality," uses a special helmet and sensors on your hands. You enter a three-dimensional world and interact with computer-generated images.

▽ IN THE FUTURE, using virtual reality equipment, you could choose your own "dream event" to participate in. *Below*, a modern player competes in bicycling event at the 1896 Olympics. Later, he'll probably mount the winner's rostrum to accept a gold medal.

Wrestling and fighting, ancient Greece

TIMELINE

B.C.

c.8000 Arrowheads dating from this time suggest hunting with bow and arrow.

c.6500 First known sledge, Finland.

c.5000 Type of bowling game in what became Egypt, in which ball is rolled toward target.

c.3800 Running rituals at Memphis (Egypt).

c.3600 Chinese emperors begin to make their subjects exercise daily with weights.

c.3100 Polo in India.

c.3000 First skis.

c.2700 Sumerian wrestling and boxing. First chariots.

c.2600 Tumbling (acrobatics) in China as religious rite.

c.2050 Curved sticks used for hitting ball, Egypt.

c.2000 Bull leaping practiced by Minoans in Crete. Tailteann Games in Ireland.

c.1550 First chariot races held in Greece.

c.1400 Hercules said to have founded Olympics.

c.1360 Fencing with sticks, Egypt.

776 Beginning of official count of ancient Greek Olympic Games, with one event, the stadion, a sprint.

724 Introduction of diaulos (double race) in 14th Olympics.

720 Introduction of dolichos (long-distance race) in 15th Olympics.

708 Introduction of wrestling and pentathlon in 18th Olympics.

688 Introduction of boxing in 23rd Olympics.

680 Introduction of chariot racing in 25th Olympics.

648 Introduction of pancration and horse-racing in 33rd Olympics.

632 Introduction of boys' contests in 37th Olympics.

586 First Isthmian Games, at Corinth.

582 First Pythian Games, at Delphi.

573 First Nemean Games.

520 First race in armor at 65th Olympics.

c.500 Hockey-like game played in Greece.

490 Athenian courier Pheidippedes runs from the Plain of Marathon to Athens to announce victory over the Persians, a distance of 24 miles (38.6 km).

468 Olympics extended to five days.

c.400 Game of kick-ball played in China.

c.200 Chinese soldiers have to pass tests of weight lifting to get into the army.

152 Leonidas becomes greatest Olympian in history, winning his 12th crown in 4 Games.

36 Competitive swimming introduced in Japanese schools.

23 Sumo wrestling begins in Japan.

6 Boulder weighing 680 lb (308 kg) said to have been thrown one-handed over his head by athlete Bybon.

A.D.

c.300 Rowing regatta held in Venice.

393 Last of ancient Greek Olympic Games (banned a year later by Roman Emperor Theodosius I).

c.400 Maya Indians' religious ball game played in what is now Mexico.

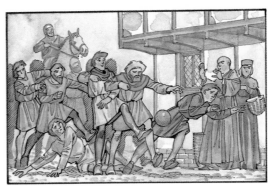
Mob soccer in London c.1300

510 Emperor Justinian forbids athletic sports, identified by Christians with the worship of Olympian gods.

c.530 Earliest written reference to skiing mentions Skridfinnar (sliding Finns), as the Lapps of Scandinavia were known.

c.1100 Jousting tournaments in France and England.

1174 First modern horse race, at Smithfield, in London.

1180 First account of ice skating, in England.

c.1200 Pelota played in France.

1206 Birch Leg Race introduced in Sweden a cross-country ski race to commemorate how 2 skiers saved the 2-year-old son of the king from the enemy.

c.1250 First illustration of bat-and-ball game resembling cricket appears in England.

1299 Bowling green is opened in Southampton, England, now world's oldest.

1314 King Edward II bans "hustling over large balls." Mob soccer played in the streets of London.

1396 Earliest known illustration of leisure skating, in Holland.

c.1410 Calcio, a form of soccer, played in Italy.

1429 Earliest reference to billiards, suggesting it was originally played on grass in France.

1457 Golf banned in Scotland, one of the first mentions of the game.

c.1466 First gun club opens in Switzerland.

c.1500 Martial art now

English cricketer Lord Hawke (1860-1938)

known as karate developed in Japan. Long-handled racket introduced.

1554 Trotting races

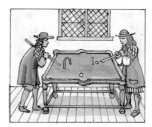
Billiards, c.1700

first held, in Holland.

1618 James I of England issues declaration to encourage "lawful recreation."

1715 Sculling race instituted, Doggett's Coat and Badge, for Thames watermen – still held.

1740 Oldest world championship of any sport founded, for real tennis.

1743 Rules drawn up in England to regulate prizefighting.

1752 The first steeplechase, run in Ireland.

1767 Skiing downhill introduced in military competition in Oslo, Norway.

1774 First rules of cricket drawn up.

1776 Beginning of modern gymnastics, in Germany.

1779 First reference to surfing on boards, Hawaiian islands.

1780 First Epsom Derby.

1781 Revival in Britain of archery.

Race in armor at Olympics in 520 B.C.

1787 Formation of MCC (Marylebone Cricket Club), regulating body of cricket.
1793 First mention of field tennis, evolving as an outdoor form of real tennis.
1817 Squash rackets developed at Harrow School, London.
1823 Rugby is first played at Rugby School, England. First speed skating contest, at Chatteris, England.
1829 First Oxford-Cambridge Boat Race.
1835 Laws of cricket drawn up.
1839 First Grand National Steeplechase held at Aintree, England.

Bicycle invented by Scot Kirkpatrick Macmillan.

First Grand National, 1839

1843 Modern skiing begins in Tromsø, Norway.
1846 Rules of association soccer drawn up at Cambridge University. First game of baseball with modern rules played in United States.
1847 First rodeo held, in New Mexico. Tenpin bowling introduced in Connecticut.
1849 Modern rules of bowls drawn up in Scotland.
1850s Annual ski meeting inaugurated in Telemark, Norway.
1851 Boat race around the Isle of Wight, England, won by U.S., leads to the founding of the America's Cup.
1855 First ice hockey match, at Kingston, Ontario, in Canada.
1858 National Association of Baseball Players is set up in United States.
1859 First walking matches staged in England.
1860 First British Open Golf Championship.
1860s Ski-jumping begins in Norway; beginning of skiing as a competitive sport.
1863 American James Plimpton makes first successful roller skate.
1865 Boxing first regulated by Queensberry Rules.
1866 First show-jumping held, in Paris. Canoeing established as a sport with the founding of the Royal Canoe Club in Britain. Australian Rules football introduced in Melbourne.
1868 First bicycle race held, in Paris.
1869 Princeton and Rutgers play first inter-collegiate football game.
1871 Rugby Union formed. Hockey rules standardized, in England.
1872 First FA Cup Final football match played.
1873 Lawn tennis introduced in England by Major W. C. Wingfield.
1875 Captain Matthew

Football, 1874

Webb first to swim the English channel.
1876 Modern rules of badminton drawn up in Poona, India.
1877 First All-England

Wimbledon, c.1880

Tennis Championships held at Wimbledon. First cricket Test match held between Australia and England, in Melbourne.
1879 First ski-jumping event held, near Oslo, Norway.
1880s Gossima, forerunner of table tennis, introduced by sporting goods manufacturers in London.
1881 First U.S. Open Tennis Championship held.
1882 Modern judo devised by Japanese teacher Jigoro Kano.
1888 Football League formed. Bobsledding developed in Switzerland.
1889 First speed skating world championships held, in Amsterdam.
1891 James Naismith devises basketball in Massachusetts.
1895 William Morgan devises volleyball in United States. First professional game of football played, in Pennsylvania. First car race held, Paris-Bordeaux-Paris.
1896 First modern Olympic Games held, in Athens.
1897 First motorcycle race held, Richmond, Surrey, England.
1903 First U.S. motorcycle race held in Brooklyn, N.Y.
1904 FIFA (Fédération Internationale de Football Association) founded.
1908 Ice skating introduced in Olympic Games. Marathon

distance standardized at 42.195 km (26.1 miles) at London Olympics.
1912 Modern pentathlon appears in Olympic Games.
1922 American Ralph Samuelson devises waterskiing, in Minnesota. Slalom skiing appears in Murren, Switzerland.
1924 First Winter Olympics, held at Chamonix, France.
1928 Olympic flame is introduced at Amsterdam Games.
1930 First football World Cup held, in Uruguay. First British Empire Games (later Commonwealth Games) held.
1936 Olympic torch relay from Greece introduced for Berlin Games.
1939 Live television broadcast of football pioneers new era in sports.
1948 First Paraplegic Games held for semi-paralyzed people, in Buckinghamshire, England. Now held every fourth year, usually in country that held the Olympic Games.
1951 First Asian Games held. First Pan-American Games held.

1954 Roger Bannister (U.K.) first to run mile in under 4 minutes (3 minutes, 59.4 seconds), at Oxford.
1955 Tae kwon do recognized as a sport in Korea.
1968 American high-jumper Dick Fosbury revolutionizes the event with his "Fosbury flop" at Mexico City Olympic Games.
1972 Terrorism at Munich Olympic Games. U.S. swimmer Mark Spitz wins record 7 gold medals at one Olympics.
1976 Black boycott of Montreal Olympic Games by 32 countries objecting to New Zealand's sports links with South Africa.
1980 United States, West Germany, and other nations boycott Moscow Olympics.
1981 International

Four-man bobsled, present day

Olympic Committee allows competitors to keep sponsorship money.
1983 First World Athletics Championships held, in Helsinki.
1984 Soviet Union and most Eastern bloc countries boycott Los Angeles Olympics.
1988 Canada's Ben Johnson, Olympic 100 meters winner, is disqualified for drug use.
1992 Remnants of Soviet Union compete in their last Olympics, in Barcelona, as "Unified Team," and head unofficial medal table.

GLOSSARY

Alpine skiing Racing downhill, either direct or down a slalom course.

Association football The original and official name for soccer.

Australian rules football A type of soccer played mainly in and around Melbourne, Australia.

Baggataway An early ball game played by North American Indians, which developed into modern lacrosse.

Battledore and shuttlecock An ancient game involving hitting a feathered piece of cork with a wooden beater used in laundries.

Bestiarii Gladiators in ancient Rome specially trained to handle and fight wild animals.

Caestus A type of ancient "knuckleduster" used by boxers and consisting of leather thongs wrapped around the fist and studded with metal buttons.

Canadian canoe A canoe propelled with a single-bladed paddle, usually from a kneeling position. See also Kayak.

Circus A great, free entertainment in ancient Rome, staged in a stadium and usually involving gladiator fights or chariot racing.

Cockfighting A cruel and ancient practice, still found in some parts of the world, in which cockerels are specially trained to tear each other to pieces for gambling and entertainment.

Decathlon An athletic event for men, consisting of ten track and field events contested over two days.

Downhill skiing A ski race down a set course.

Drag hunting A form of hunting, on horseback or on foot, in which the hounds follow a trail laid with an artificial scent, and no killing is involved.

Drag racing A motor sport in which pairs of specially-built cars or motorcycles are raced over a 400 m track from a standing start.

Fives One of a number of ball games in which players hit a small ball against a wall with gloved hands; handball.

Gladiators Trained fighters in ancient Rome, drawn from slaves, criminals, and prisoners of war, who fought in amphitheaters with a variety of weapons for the entertainment of the people.

Grand Prix French for "big prize" – a term used for certain important races in car or motorcycle racing.

Heptathlon An athletic event for women consisting of seven track and field events contested over two days.

Jousting Mock battles of the Middle Ages between knights fighting with lances, swords, and other weapons.

Kayak An enclosed canoe paddled in a sitting position with a double-bladed paddle. See also Canadian canoe.

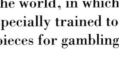

Luge A toboggan ridden on the back.

Martial arts One-to-one combat sports designed originally to train men for war.

Nordic skiing The ski sports including cross-country racing, ski-jumping, and biathlon.

Outrigger In rowing, an iron bracket fixed to the outside of the boat. It extends the rowlock, which holds the oar, giving greater leverage. Also the name of a Pacific sea-fishing boat.

Pancration A combat event held in the ancient Greek Olympics in which contestants were allowed to punch, kick, knee, and strangle each other until only one was left standing.

Pentathlon An event or sport with five parts. The ancient Greek pentathlon consisted of long jump, discus, sprint, javelin, and wrestling. Modern pentathlon consists of riding, fencing, pistol shooting, swimming, and cross-country running. See Decathlon; Heptathlon.

Photo finish A method for judging close finishes to races, using a continuous film moving across a slit facing the finishing line. The photo also shows the times of the runners.

Prizefighting The bare-knuckle combat sport, often staged illegally, that developed into modern boxing.

Rackets The stringed bats used in sports such as tennis, but also the name of a game similar to squash.

Real, or royal, tennis An old form of tennis, still played on special courts.

Regatta A sailing or rowing race meet.

Sculling Rowing with an oar in each hand.

Skeleton toboggan A toboggan ridden on the stomach.

Slalom A course, as in skiing or conoeing, in which contestants have to zigzag around obstacles.

Stadion A sprint race in ancient Greece. The distance, a "stade," which give its name to the race and hence to the place where it was held (stadium), was 630 feet (192 m) at Olympia.

Standing jumps Events held in the early modern Olympics in which contestants jumped (long, high, and triple jump) from a standing start.

Starting blocks Devices on the track that help sprinters push off at the start.

Steeplechase A horse race with obstacles, run over 2 miles (3.2 km) or more. Also the name of track races that include fixed hurdles and a water jump.

Sumo wrestling A Japanese sport, full of ritual, in which contestants try to put their opponent on the floor or out of the ring. A bout rarely lasts more than a few seconds.

Toboggan See Luge; Skeleton toboggan.

Torch race A relay race in ancient Greece staged as a religious ritual. The modern Olympic torch relay derives from this.

INDEX

Illustrations are shown in bold type.

A

advertising 36
amateurs 28, 33
amphitheaters 10, **10**
animals in sports 18-19
archery 14, **14**, **17**, 44
Aztecs 12, **12**

B

badminton **22**, 45
baggataway 12
Bannister, Roger **30**, 45
baseball **17**, 21, 45
basketball **21**, 45
bestiarii 11
bicycle racing **25**, **36**, 45
Bikila, Abebe **31**
billiards **16**, 44
blood sports 17, 18
bobsled **35**, 45
bowls **15**, 44, 45
boxing 7, **24**, 45
boycotts, Olympic 33, 45
bullfighting **19**
bull leaping 7, **7**, 44

C

Campbell, Donald 38, 39
Campbell, Malcolm 38, **38**, 39
car racing 25, **25**, 38, 40-41, **40-41**, 42, 45
chariot racing 9, **9**, 11, 44
Circus Maximus **11**
cockfighting **18**, 46
Coe, Sebastian **32**
Colosseum 10
Comaneci, Nadia **32**
Compton, Dennis **30**

cricket **16**, **21**, 29, **36**, **41**, 44, 45
curling **35**

D

Dempsey, Jack **28**
Didrikson, Mildred "Babe" **27**
disabled people 37
diving **26**
Dod, Lottie **27**
Doggett's Coat and Badge **17**, 44
D'Oliveira, Basil **31**
drug use 37
dueling 24

E, F

Earthball **43**
Ederle, Gertrude 27, **27**
Egypt (ancient) 6

falconry **19**
fencing **15**, 44
football 20, **37**, **40**, 45
fox hunting **18**

G

gladiators **10**, 10-11, 43, 46
golf **16**, **41**, **42**, 44, 45
Grand National 18
Greece (ancient) 8, 9, 26
gymnastics **22**, 44

H

Hagen, Walter **28**
hare coursing **18**
Heiden, Eric **34**
Henie, Sonja **27**, **34**
Hitler, Adolph 29, **29**
horses 18-19, **18-19**, 44, 45
hunting 6, 16, 18, 44

I

ice hockey **35**, **36**, 45
ice skating 15, 34, **35**, 44, 45
industrial revolution 17

J

jai alai **38**
Johnson, Ben **37**, 45
Jones, Bobby **28**
jousting 14, **14**, 44, 46

K

kayak **26**
kendo 13
keretizen 8
kite-flying **13**
kolven 16
kyudo 13

L

land speed record (LSR) 38-39
Laver, Rod **31**
Layynina, Larissa **30**
Louis, Joe **30**
Lycra **40**

M

Maradona, Diego **37**
martial arts 13
Matthews, Stanley **30**
Mayas 12
McEnroe, John **36**, 37
Middle Ages 14
Minoans 7
Moore, Bobby **31**
motorcycle racing 25, **25**, 45
Muldowney, Shirley 27

N, O

New Games 43
ninepins 24
North American Indians 12, **12**
Nurmi, Paavo **28**

Olympia 8-9, **8-9**
Olympics 8, 22, 23, 26, 29, 32-33, **32-33**, 34, **43**, 44, 45
Olympic torch **29**
Onishchenko, Boris **32**

P

pancration 9, 44
Paralympics 37
Pelé **31**
pell-mell 16
politics in sports 29
polo 7, 18, **21**, 44
prizefighting 17, **17**, 44
professionals 28
Puritans 16, 17

Q, R

Queensberry rules 24, 45

rackets **15**, **17**, **41**, **42**
real tennis 15, 44, 45
religion 6, 8
Renaissance 15
Robinson, Jackie 30, **30**
Rome (ancient) 10-11
rowing 17, **26**, 44
rugby 20, **20**, 45
Ruth, Babe **28**

S

sailing 26
sculling 26
show-jumping 19

N, O (skates)

skates **41**
skeleton tobogganing **35**
skiing **6**, 17, 34, **34**, 44, 45
ski-jumping **34**, 45
soccer 14, 16, 20, **40**, 44, 45, 46
Soviet Union 30, 33, 45
speed skating 34, 45
sponsorship 33
starting blocks **33**
starting pistol **33**
sumo wrestling **13**, 44
swimming 26, **26**, 44
swordplay 15

T

Tailteann Games 7
tennis 22, **41**, 45
tenpin bowling 24, 45
terrorism 32, 45
tiger hunting **19**
Tilden, Bill **28**
Torvill and Dean **34**
Tunney, Gene **28**
Tyson, Mike **37**

V

virtual reality **43**, **43**

W, Y

Washington, Kenny 30, **30**
water speed record (WSR) 38-39
water sports 26
Webb, Matthew **26**, 45
Weissmuller, Johnny **28**
Wimbledon 23, 45
winter sports 34-35
women in sports 27
World Cup 29, 45
World War II 30
wrestling **6**

yacht racing 26